More Word Games

By the same authors
Word Games

Published by arrangement with the British Broadcasting Corporation

More Word Games

Sandy Brownjohn and Janet Whitaker

Illustrated by Toni Goffe

HODDER AND STOUGHTON
LONDON   SYDNEY   AUCKLAND   TORONTO

D655159

ISBN 0 340 38133 7 (Bds)
ISBN 0 340 36013 5 (Pbk)

First published 1985
Selection and arrangement copyright © 1985 Sandy
Brownjohn and Janet Whitaker

All rights reserved. No part of this publication may be
reproduced or transmitted in any form or by any means,
electronic or mechanical, including photocopy, recording,
or any information storage and retrieval system, without
permission in writing from the publisher.

Printed and bound in Hong Kong for
Hodder and Stoughton Educational,
a division of Hodder and Stoughton Ltd,
Mill Road, Dunton Green, Sevenoaks, Kent,
by Colorcraft Ltd
Photoset in Univers Medium by
Rowland Phototypesetting Ltd,
Bury St Edmunds, Suffolk

Contents

Introduction	6
Tongue Twisters	7
One Waggly Walrus	10
As Sick as a Parrot	12
Similes	14
The Furniture Game	16
Metaphor	18
Water Picture	20
Who? What? Where? How?	22
Riddles	25
More Riddles	26
One for Sorrow, Two for Joy	28
The Name of the Game	30
The Key of the Kingdom	32
Locked in the Lavatory	36
Whistlestop!	39
Night Mail	40
Oranges and Lemons	42
Machines	43
To Plough and Sow, to Reap and Mow	44
Work	45
Orange, Silver, Sausage	47
Rhyme	50
Mime the Rhyme	52
King Foo Foo	53
Half-time	54
Rhyme-time	55
Mutton Pies	57
Glossary of Terms	60
Index of Poems (Titles and First Lines)	61
Index of Poets	63
Acknowledgments	64

Introduction

Word Games started life as a series of BBC School Radio programmes. Sandy wrote them and Janet produced them. For those of you who enjoy playing games, in this book you will find a bran tub into which you can dip at will.

You will find party games, jokes, invented words, puns, rhymes and wordplay of all kinds that you can try out with your friends. There are poems and songs, too, which we chose because we liked the way the poets had enjoyed using the language.

There is no need to read this book from front to back, or even from back to front, just open it anywhere and enjoy playing with words. See what you can do with them. You'll be surprised.

We should like to thank all those who have helped *Word Games* on its way. Particular thanks go to Denise Coffey, Vicky Ireland and Ken Shanley, the actors, who made the scripts come alive and, we hope, had fun in the process. Thanks also are due to Janet Maybin, Marion Conry and Yvonne Klemperer for the work they put in on the programmes and the books. Last, but definitely not least, a special thanks to Diana Simons, possibly the best editor in the business!

Sandy Brownjohn and *Janet Whitaker*

Tongue Twisters

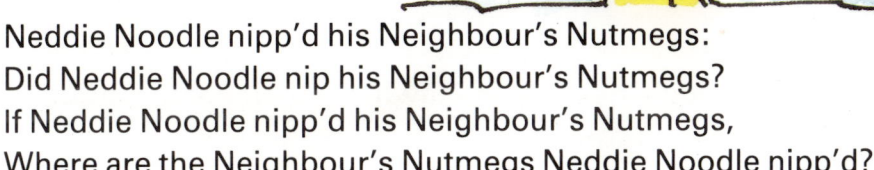

Neddie Noodle nipp'd his Neighbour's Nutmegs:
Did Neddie Noodle nip his Neighbour's Nutmegs?
If Neddie Noodle nipp'd his Neighbour's Nutmegs,
Where are the Neighbour's Nutmegs Neddie Noodle nipp'd?

I want to be a wallaby,
A wallaby like Willoughby.
When will I be a wallaby
Like Willoughby the wallaby?

Colin West

Swan swam over the sea,
Swim swan swim.
Swan swam back again;
Well swum swan.

Word Game
Make up some tongue twisters of your own. Choose a letter of the alphabet and try to begin as many words as possible with it. Your sentences must make sense!

The Far Famed Fairy Tale of Fenella

A Famous Fish Factor Found himself Father of Five Fine Flirting Females, Fanny, Florence, Fernanda, Francesca, and Fenella. The First Four were Flattering, Flat Featured, Forbidden Faced, Freckled Frumps; Fretful, Flippant, Foolish, and Full of Fun. The Fisher Failed, and was Forced by Fickle Fortune to Forego his Footman, Forfeit his Forefather's Fine Fields, and Find a Forlorn Farmhouse in a Forsaken Forest. The Four Fretful Females, Fond of Figuring at Feasts in Feathers and Fashionable Finery, Fumed at their Fugitive Father, Forsaken by Fulsome, Flattering Fortune hunters, who Followed them when Fish Flourished. Fenella Fondled her Father, Flavoured their Food, Forgot her Flattering Followers, and Frolicked in Frieze without Flounces. The Father, Finding himself Forced to Forage in Foreign parts For a Fortune, Found he could afford a Fairing to his Five Fondlings. The First Four were Fain to Foster their Frivolity with Fine Frills and Fans, Fit to Finish their Father's Finances. Fenella, Fearful of Flooring him,

Formed a Fancy For a Full Fresh Flower. Fate Favoured the Fish Factor For a Few days, when he Fell in with a Frog. His Faithful Filly's Footsteps Faltered, and Food Failed. He Found himself in Front of a Fortified Fortress. Finding it Forsaken, and Feeling himself Feeble and Forlorn, with Feasting, he Fed upon the Fish, Flesh and Fowl he Found, Fricasseed and Fried, and when Full, Fell Flat on his Face on the Floor. Fresh in the Forenoon he Forthwith Flew to the Fruitful Fields, and not Forgetting Fenella, he Filched a Fair Flower, when a Foul, Frightful, Fiendish Figure Flashed Forth. "Felonious Feller, Fingering my Flower, I'll Finish you! Go! Say Farewell to your Fine Felicitous Family, and Face me in a Fortnight!" The Faint-hearted Fisher Fumed and Faltered, and Fast was Far in his Flight. His Five daughters Flew to Fall at his Feet, and Fervently Felicitate him. Frantically and Fluently he unfolded his Fate; Fenella, Forthwith Fortified by Filial Fondness, Followed her Father's Footsteps, and Flung her Faultless Form at the Foot of the Frightful Figure, who Forgave the Father, and Fell Flat on his Face; For he had Fervently Fallen in a Fiery Fit of love For the Fair Fenella. He Feasted and Fostered her, till Fascinated by his Faithfulness, she Forgot the Ferocity of his Face, Form, and Feature, and Finally, Frankly, and Fondly Fixed Friday, the Fifth day of February For the affair to come off. There were present at the wedding, Fanny, Florence, Fernanda, Francesca, and the Fisher; there was Festivity, Fragrance, Finery, Fireworks, Fricasseed Frogs, Fritters, Fish, Flesh, Fowls, and Furmity, Frontinac, Flip, and Fare, Fit For the Fastidious, Fruit, Fuss, Flambeaux, and Flowers, Four Fat Fiddlers and Fifers, and the Frightful Form of the Fortunate and Frumpish Fiend Fell From him, and he Fell at Fenella's Feet, a Fair Favoured, Fine, Frank Freeman of the Forest. Behold the Fruits of Filial affection!!

One Waggly Walrus

Word Game
Write a sentence for each number from 1 to 10 using ALLITERATION. Make as many words as possible in each sentence begin with the same sound as the number. If you use a dictionary you will find more unusual sounding words to put in your sentences. Read them out loud to each other and enjoy the sound of them.

Did You Know?
Tongue twisters use ALLITERATION, or words that begin with the same sound. The expression *Tongue Twisters* is itself ALLITERATIVE.

One waggly walrus won a wet wager,
Two trustful twins tumbled into a typhoon.
Three thin thoroughbreds thumped a thick thief,
Four fiddly ferns ferociously ate a ferret,
Five fervent fleas sat famished in a farm,
Six shy shuttlecocks swam in shampoo.
Seven stupid strawberries sinned on a stripey stretcher,
Eight echoing earthquakes exterminated an eclipse,
Nine nosy nomads knitted knotted knickers,
Ten topless toffees told a tale.

Did You Know? The Anglo-Saxons used ALLITERATION in their poems. A famous long poem tells the story of the hero Beowulf who comes face to face with a dragon in one of his adventures.

. . . and out of the barrow broke
a stream surging through it, a stream of fire with waves of deadly flame; . . .
. . . Straightaway
the breath of the dragon billowed from the rock in a hissing gust; the ground boomed.
The temper of the twisted tangle-thing was fired to close now in battle.
It came flowing forward, flaming and coiling, rushing on its fate.

Word Games
Write your own dragon using ALLITERATION.   Or you might write about other animals in the same way.

My dragon breathes and belches out
Blistering, burning bellows and blasts.
His teeth are tremendous and terrible

And his noisy nostrils
Flourish fierce and ferocious flames of fiery flux.

As Sick as a Parrot

My girl's a corker, she's a New Yorker,
I'd give her anything to keep her in style,
She's got a mop of hair, just like a grizzly bear,
That's where the money always goes.

She's got a pair of eyes just like two custard pies . . .

She's got a runny nose just like a fireman's hose . . .

She's got a pair of lips just like two greasy chips . . .

She's got a pair of hips just like two battleships . . .

She's got a pair of feet just like two plates of meat . . .

Did You Know? When you describe a thing by saying it is 'like' something else, you are using a SIMILE. You are saying it is similar to something else:
As wet as a fish – as dry as a bone;
As live as a bird – as dead as a stone;
As hard as flint – as soft as a mole;
As white as a lily – as black as coal.

Word Game
There are many sayings that use SIMILES.
How many can you collect?
As strong as a horse – as weak as a kitten;
As blind as a bat – as wise as an owl.
Why not make up some of your own?

Word Game
Create an animal using SIMILES to describe what it would be like.

How a Good Greyhound is Shaped

He needs
A head like a snake, a neck like a drake,
A back like a beam, a belly like a bream,
A foot like a cat, and a tail like a rat.

Traditional

How to Make a Bear

He needs
A coat like thick brown moss,
A head like a sculptured rock,
Claws like metal combs,
Paws like boxing gloves,
And a growl like rumbling thunder.

Anonymous

Similes

Imagine

Imagine a snail
As big as a whale,
Imagine a lark
As big as a shark,
Imagine a bee
As big as a tree.
Imagine a toad
As long as a road,
Imagine a hare
As big as a chair,
Imagine a goat
As long as a boat
And a flea the same size as me.

Roland Egan

When you use SIMILES you are using your imagination to compare two very different things. SIMILES help you to build up interesting pictures in your mind. What would the world look like to other creatures? SIMILES can help you to imagine that.

The Fly

How large unto the tiny fly
Must little things appear!
– A rosebud like a feather bed,
Its prickle like a spear,
A dewdrop like a looking-glass
A hair like golden wire;
The smallest grain of mustard-seed
As fierce as coals of fire;
A loaf of bread, a lofty hill;
A wasp, a cruel leopard;
And specks of salt as bright to see
As lambkins to a shepherd.

Walter de la Mare

Frogs

Frogs sit more solid
Than anything sits. In mid-leap they are
Parachutists falling
In a free fall. They die on roads
With arms across their chests and
Heads high.

I love frogs that sit
Like Buddha, that fall without
Parachutes, that die
Like Italian tenors.
Above all, I love them because,
Pursued in water, they never
Panic so much that they fail
To make stylish triangles
With their ballet dancer's
Legs.

Norman MacCaig

Word Game

How many interesting SIMILES can you find to describe a person, animal or place which you know very well? You might want to write them down in a poem.

The Furniture Game

From You're the Top!

You're the top!
You're the Colosseum.
You're the top!
You're the Louvre Museum.
You're a melody from a symphony by Strauss,
You're a Bendel bonnet,
A Shakespeare sonnet,
You're Mickey Mouse.
You're the Nile,
You're the Tow'r of Pisa,
You're the smile
On the Mona Lisa.
I'm a worthless check, a total wreck, a flop,
But if, Baby, I'm the bottom,
You're the top!

You're the top!
You're Mahatma Gandhi.
You're the top!
You're Napoleon brandy.
You're the purple light of a summer night in Spain,
You're the National Gall'ry,
You're Garbo's sal'ry,
You're cellophane.
You're sublime,
You're a turkey dinner,
You're the time
Of the Derby winner.
I'm a toy balloon that is fated soon to pop,
But if, Baby, I'm the bottom
You're the top!

Cole Porter

Word Game
You can play the FURNITURE GAME with a group of friends. *You* think of someone in the group and the others have to guess who it is. They do this by asking questions like –
What piece of furniture is this person?
What animal? What time of day? What colour? What item of clothing?
You must answer with the first thing that comes into your head. The others should be able to guess who it is from your answers.

Word Game
Another way of playing the Furniture Game is for everyone in a group to write his or her name on a piece of paper. All the pieces of paper are folded and collected in a hat. You must write about the person whose name you drew out of the hat. Ask yourself questions and write down the answers. Try to be adventurous in your answers. Make sure you say the person IS something else. DO NOT say he or she is LIKE something else.
When you have finished read out your descriptions and try to guess whom each has written about.

She's an anxious kingfisher,
She's purple.
If placed in a raging river she becomes an aluminium canoe.
She stands out to the world as a dining room table,
She's the cold of Alaska and the warmth of Italy,
She's a fox
And a five bar gate.
She's Irish coffee and also vodka.
If she were a boot she'd be trampling down the rubbish.
She's a country pub in Dorset
And she's the sprinter who works for her crowd.

Metaphor

Did You Know? When you play the Furniture Game you are using METAPHORS. When you say someone *is* something else you are using a METAPHOR.

> The moon's a big white football
> The sun's a pound of butter,
> The earth is going round the twist
> And I'm a little nutter!
>
> *Kit Wright*

This is very different from using a simile when you would say 'The moon's like a big white football.'
To be *like* 'a big white football' is very different from *actually being* 'a big white football'.
Of course, the moon is *not* actually 'a big white football', but in our imaginations anything is possible. You can do anything with words.
The picture, or *image*, you create is much more vivid and exciting when you use METAPHORS. This is one of the most lively and imaginative ways of using language.

Cleaning Ladies

Belly stuffed with dust and fluff,
The Hoover moos and drones,
Grazing down on the carpet pasture:
Cow with electric bones.

Up in the tree of a chair the cat
Switches off its purr,
Stretches, blinks: a neat pink tongue
Vacuum cleans its fur.

Kit Wright

The Beach

The beach is a quarter of golden fruit,
a soft ripe melon
sliced to a half-moon curve,
having a thick green rind
of jungle growth;
and the sea devours it
with its sharp white teeth.

W. Hart-Smith

Word Game

Can you describe something using METAPHORS? Choose one of the seasons (Spring, Summer, Autumn, Winter) and ask yourself questions like those in the Furniture Game. You can build up a picture of your season through the *images* in your mind. You might even take just one image and write about your season using all the words you can think of that belong to your METAPHOR.

Summer

Summer is a *cigarette*
Inhaled until it has nothing left to give,
And the *charred* remains are left to make
The *smoky* pillar of Autumn.

Mark Nathan

You could try writing about other things in this way – like 'The Beach' poem printed opposite.

The Sea

The sea is a hungry dog,
Giant and grey.
He rolls on the beach all day.
With his clashing teeth and shaggy jaws
Hour upon hour he gnaws
The rumbling, tumbling stones,
And 'Bones, bones, bones, bones!'
The giant sea-dog moans,
Licking his greasy paws.

And when the night wind roars
And the moon rocks in the stormy cloud,
He bounds to his feet and snuffs and sniffs,
Shaking his wet sides over the cliffs,
And howls and hollos long and loud.

But on quiet days in May or June,
When even the grasses on the dune
Play no more their reedy tune,
With his head between his paws
He lies on the sandy shores,
So quiet, so quiet, he scarcely snores.

James Reeves

Water Picture

In the pond in the park
all things are double:
Long buildings hang and
wriggle gently. Chimneys
are bent legs bouncing
on clouds below. A flag
wags like a fishhook
down there in the sky.

The arched stone bridge
is an eye, with underlid
in the water. In its lens
dip crinkled heads with hats
that don't fall off. Dogs go by,
barking on their backs.
A baby, taken to feed the
ducks, dangles upside-down,
a pink balloon for a buoy.

Treetops deploy a haze of
cherry bloom for roots,
where birds coast belly-up
in the glass bowl of a hill;
from its bottom a bunch
of peanut-munching children
is suspended by their
sneakers, waveringly.

A swan, with twin necks
forming the figure three,
steers between two dimpled
towers doubled. Fondly
hissing, she kisses herself,
and all the scene is troubled:
water-windows splinter,
tree-limbs tangle, the bridge
folds like a fan.

May Swenson

Who? What? Where? How?

Inquisitiveness

Please, how does one spell *definite*?
Has it a double f in it?

Please, how old was Euripides?
And where are the Antipodes?

Please, what is a delphinium?
And whence comes aluminium?

Please, where does one find phosphorus?
And how big is the Bosporus?

Please, why are you so furious?
Do tell me, I'm so curious!

Colin West

I often wonder why, oh why,
All grown-ups say to me:
'When you are old and six foot high,
What do you want to be?'

I sometimes wonder what they'd say
If I should ask them all
What *they* would like to be, if they
Were six years old and small.

Raymond Wilson

Word Game
Write down five questions on a piece of paper. Get your friend to write five of his own. Any questions will be suitable, like 'Where does the rainbow end?' or 'Who pinched the sugar?' Swap questions with your friend and answer each other's questions. Be as inventive and unusual as you can in your answers.

Questions

What is the sun?
– The blushing face of the universe.

Where does the sky begin?
– Just above the smoke of the factory chimneys.

How do you cut the air?
– With the wind.

What's inside a hill?
– Things to come up in the future.

When is the end of time?
– When the last cuckoo sinks into Hell.

Intelligence Test

'What do you use your eyes for?'
The white-coated man enquired.
'I use my eyes for looking,'
Said Toby, 'unless I'm tired.'

'I see. And then you close them,'
Observed the white-coated man.
'Well done. A very good answer.
Let's try another one.

'What is your nose designed for?
What use is the thing to you?'
'I use my nose for smelling,'
Said Toby, 'don't you too?'

'I do indeed,' said the expert,
'That's what the thing is for.
Now I've another question to ask you,
Then there won't be any more.

'What are your ears intended for?
Those things at each side of your head?
Come on – don't be shy – I'm sure you can say.'
'For washing behind,' Toby said.

Vernon Scannell

Mirror Poem

If I look within the mirror,
Deep inside its frozen tears,
Shall I see the man I'll marry
    Standing at my shoulder,
    Leaning down the years?

Shall I smile upon the mirror,
Shall my love look, smiling, back?
Midnight on midsummer's eve:
    What becomes of marriage
    If the glass should crack?

Kit Wright

Riddles – for budding detectives

The Riddle of the Sphinx

What has one voice,
And goes on four legs in the morning
Two legs in the afternoon,
And three legs in the evening?

(Answer – A man)

Did You Know? This is one of the oldest riddles in the world. The Sphinx was a fabulous beast with the head of a woman and the body of a lion. She used to ask everyone who passed by if they could solve this riddle. If they were unable to answer she would eat them or push them over the cliff on which she sat.

It is in the rock but not in the stone,
It is in the marrow but not in the bone,
It is in the bolster but not in the bed,
It is not in the living nor yet in the dead.

(Answer – The letter R)

Word Game
Riddles have a magic quality. They hide secrets which you have to guess. There are different kinds of riddles. Some use pairs of words which go together – 'rock' and 'stone', 'marrow' and 'bone'.
Write your own riddle using pairs of words. Use rhyme, too, if you can. The first words of each pair will contain letters which spell the answer to your riddle. Ask your friends to guess the answer.

More Riddles

My first is in *b*ook but not in cover,
My second in *si*ster but not in brother,
My third is in *r*ain but not in sun,
My fourth is in brea*d* but not in bun,
My whole is a creature. Watch me fly,
Soaring into an azure sky.

I was round and small like a pearl,
Then long and slender and brave as an earl,
Since, like a hermit, I lived in a cell,
And now, like a rogue, in the wide world I dwell.

In marble walls as white as milk,
Lined with a skin as soft as silk;
Within a fountain crystal clear,
A golden apple doth appear.
No doors there are to this stronghold –
Yet thieves break in and steal the gold.

Traditional

(Answer – An egg)

(Answer – First an egg,
Then a silkworm,
Then a cocoon,
Lastly, a moth.)

On the way a miracle: water became bone.

(Answer – Ice)

Riddles often sound magical. Things seem to happen that do not sound possible. When you describe something in this way you can use METAPHORS (see page 18).

Word Game

SUPERSLEUTH – lay a trail of interesting clues to describe something. Write them down as a riddle. You must not give the game away too easily so try to describe your subject in unusual ways. You might use METAPHORS, like the two riddles here – saying that a thing *is* something else.

Word Game

Write another riddle where you imagine that you are the thing you are writing about. Imagine how it would feel to be this thing, as well as describing what you look like. The Anglo-Saxons were masters of this kind of riddle. Notice how vivid and exciting the language is in the riddle opposite.

I will Give my Love an Apple

I will give my love an apple, without e'er a core
I will give my love a house without e'er a door,
I will give my love a palace wherein she may be
And she may unlock it without e'er a key.

My head is the apple without e'er a core,
My mind is the house without e'er a door,
My heart is the palace wherein she may be
And she may unlock it without e'er a key.

Traditional

My breast is puffed up and my neck is swollen.
I've a fine head and a high waving tail,
ears and eyes also but only one foot;
a long neck, a strong beak, a back and
two sides, and a rod right through my middle.
My home is high above men. When he who moves
the forest molests me, I suffer a great deal of misery.
Scourged by the rainlash, I stand alone;
I'm bruised by heavy batteries of hail,
hoar-frost attacks and snow half-hides me.
I must endure all this, not pour out my misery.

(Answer – A weathercock)

One for Sorrow, Two for Joy

Solomon Grundy, born on Monday
Christened on Tuesday, married on Wednesday
Took ill on Thursday, worse on Friday
Died on Saturday, buried on Sunday
That was the end of Solomon Grundy.

Monday's child is fair of face,
Tuesday's child is full of grace,
Wednesday's child is full of woe,
Thursday's child has far to go,
Friday's child is loving and giving,
Saturday's child works hard for a living,
But the child that is born on the Sabbath day
Is bonny and blithe and good and gay.

One for sorrow, two for joy,
three for a wedding, four for a boy,
five for silver, six for gold,
seven for a secret never to be told.

Have You Noticed? Many poems and rhymes are written to a pattern. Sometimes they are based on numbers, sometimes on days of the week or months of the year. There are also patterns that are repeated throughout a poem, like 'The House that Jack Built'.

> **Word Game**
> Write a pattern poem which is a list, using numbers, days of the week, months of the year, or any other set of things you like.

This is the house that Jack built.
This is the malt that lay in the house that Jack built.
This is the rat that ate the malt that lay in the house that Jack built.
This is the cat that killed the rat that ate the malt
that lay in the house that Jack built.
This is the dog that chased the cat that killed the rat that ate the malt
that lay in the house that Jack built.
This is the cow with the crumpled horn that worried the dog
that chased the cat that killed the rat that ate the malt
that lay in the house that Jack built.
This is the maiden all forlorn that milked the cow
with the crumpled horn that worried the dog
that chased the cat that killed the rat that ate the malt
that lay in the house that Jack built.
This is the man all tattered and torn
that kissed the maiden all forlorn
that milked the cow with the crumpled horn
that worried the dog that chased the cat that killed the rat
that ate the malt that lay in the house that Jack built.

The Name of the Game

The Class

Ten-ton Tina's staring,
Tracey's passing notes,
Bob is wetting Luna's shoe
Seeing if it floats.
Ethel broke the microscope,
Teacher's in a rage,
Egghead's sitting calmly
Wise as any sage.
Baby Beth is squealing,
Crying, turning pink,
Soppy Sam is dipping
Laura's plaits in ink.
Kirk and Spock are fighting
Underneath the table,
Buster Jones is pinching,
Hitting when he's able.
Beanpole Dave is crawling
'Cross the floor Red Injun style,
Grim Headmaster's watching
Glaring all the while.

Rachel Meyers

Word Game
This is another 'list' poem. Choose a situation, e.g. a football crowd, school dinnertime, assembly, playtime, a party. Make a list of people's names and write one (or two) lines about each person. Each small detail contributes to the effect of the whole poem and gives you a picture of what is happening. In a humorous poem rhyme can be useful. Try to choose names that are not of people you know. It can be fun to collect names from the telephone directory.

Funeral

Barbra looks longingly at the lamp shade,
Mrs Ryestone stares covetously at the china.
Mr Stails tries not to see the priceless antique vase.
David loads his car, muttering about 'what a wonderful woman she was'.
Sarah packs potted plants into bags,
Anne reaches out for the rabbit picture,
John and Gerry argue over the portrait of her husband,
The boy next door nips in, in time to remove garden tools and furniture.
Carol stuffs cakes and cooking utensils into shopping bags.
Mr Ridley removes the flowers into a milk bottle
And makes off with the vase.
Emma and Mary divide the jewellery,
Mr Royce searches the bookshelves,
Saskia and Lucy sob in the garden.

Kefi Beswick

Word Game

You can play the same game but make your poem serious. Choose a suitable subject, e.g. people on a train, a bus queue, a church congregation, a jury. The following poem looks at people's behaviour after a funeral. Most of them seem only to be thinking of what they can take from the dead woman's belongings. Notice that rhyme is not used here.

The Key of the Kingdom

In This City...

In this city, perhaps a street.
In this street, perhaps a house.
In this house, perhaps a room
And in this room a woman sitting,
Sitting in the darkness, sitting and crying
For someone who has just gone through the door
And who has just switched off the light
Forgetting she was there.

Alan Brownjohn

Word Game
This is another sort of pattern. This pattern is a picture within a picture, within a picture. Write a poem which has a pattern. Make it like a flight of stairs, like 'The Key of the Kingdom' which goes from the key of the kingdom to a basket of sweet flowers and then back again. You might like to try going from a mountain to a grain of sand, or silence to the loudest noise and back again.

This is the key of the kingdom:
In that kingdom there is a city;
In that city is a town;
In that town there is a street;
In that street there winds a lane;
In that lane there is a yard;
In that yard there is a house;
In that house there waits a room;
In that room an empty bed;
And on that bed a basket –
A basket of sweet flowers:
    Of flowers, of flowers;
    A basket of sweet flowers.

Flowers in a basket;
Basket on the bed;
Bed in the chamber;
Chamber in the house;
House in the weedy yard;
Yard in the winding lane;
Lane in the broad street;
Street in the high town;
Town in the city;
City in the kingdom –
This is the key of the kingdom,
    Of the kingdom this is the key.

Traditional

It's Winter, it's Winter

It's winter, it's winter, it's wonderful winter,
When everyone lounges around in the sun!
It's winter, it's winter, it's wonderful winter,
When everyone's brown like a steak overdone!
It's winter, it's winter, it's wonderful winter,
It's swimming and surfing and hunting for conkers!
It's winter, it's winter, it's wonderful winter,
And I am completely and utterly bonkers!

Kit Wright

Word Game

Make up your own pattern for a poem. You might decide to repeat one line at intervals through the poem. You can even do this as a group where everybody writes a verse and each verse starts with the same line.

The Song of a House

All of my attics used to sing:
Down the stairs, down the stairs
And down to the dark rooms
To see the rotting wools,
And the dusty smells of the old tattered mattresses.
Old statues and paintings show
Signs of pleasant work.

All of my windows used to sing:
Look through us, look through us,
Look, so our views are seen
And we do not get dusty.
Wash us so we are clean and fresh,
We do not care if you look in or out –
Only look, look.
If you do not look we will crack and mist.

All of my floorboards used to sing:
Walk upon me, walk upon me,
And I will creak with pleasure –
But just walk upon me, walk upon me.
Although I am old and dirty I still remain
And I will not collapse
Until my nails begin to bend,
So walk upon me, walk upon me.

All of my books used to sing:
Please read me,
Please read me –
Read me till my pages go ragged,
Read me till my story
Grows old.

        Extract from 'Lumb Song', a
        communal poem by children

Here is another kind of pattern.

Window

There once was a very small window,
hidden away in a corner of a room.

One day a small boy looked through the window
and saw a bright red fire engine.

An actress looked through the window
and saw her name in lights.

A farmer looked through the window
and saw a field of harvested wheat.

A ghost looked through the window
and saw life.

A press-man looked through the window
and saw his story on the front page.

A gardener looked through the window
and saw a mowed lawn.

Then God looked through the window
and the window broke.

Steve Webber

Locked in the Lavatory

Oh dear, what can the matter be,
Three old ladies were locked in the lavatory,
They were there from Monday to Saturday,
Nobody knew they were there.

Anonymous

Twinkle, twinkle, little bat!
How I wonder what you're at!
Up above the world you fly,
Like a tea-tray in the sky.

From *Alice's Adventures in Wonderland*
by Lewis Carroll

These two rhymes are having fun using patterns of other rhymes. Do you know the original rhymes? You may also know some playground rhymes that do the same thing.

Word Game

Find a rhyme or song you know and use its pattern to write a new poem. It can be funny, like the ones here. But you can also write a more serious poem. Sometimes they work better. On the next page the poem 'Leaves' is based on the pattern in the song 'Who killed Cock Robin?' – 'I,' said the sparrow, 'with my bow and arrow.'

The London Bus Conductor's Prayer

Our Father who art in Hendon,
Holloway be thy name.
Thy Kingston come,
Thy Wimbledon,
In Erith as it is in Epsom.
Give us this Bray our Maidenhead;
And forgive us our bypasses,
As we forgive those who bypass against us.
And lead us not into Thames Ditton.
But deliver us from Esher.
For thine is the Kingston,
The Purley and the Crawley,
For Iver and Iver,
Crouch End.

Anonymous

Leaves

Who's killed the leaves?

Me, says the apple, I've killed them all.
Fat as a bomb or a cannonball
I've killed the leaves.

Who sees them drop?

Me, says the pear, they will leave me all bare
So all the people can point and stare.
I see them drop.

Who'll catch their blood?

Me, me, me, says the marrow, the marrow.
I'll get so rotund that they'll need a wheelbarrow.
I'll catch their blood.

Who'll make their shroud?

Me, says the swallow, there's just time enough
Before I must pack all my spools and be off.
I'll make their shroud.

Who'll dig their grave?

Me, says the river, with the power of the clouds
A brown deep grave I'll dig under my floods.
I'll dig their grave.

Who'll be their parson?

Me, says the crow, for it is well-known
I study the bible right down to the bone.
I'll be their parson.

Who'll be chief mourner?

Me, says the wind, I will cry through the grass
The people will pale and go cold when I pass.
I'll be chief mourner.

Who'll carry the coffin?

Me, says the sunset, the whole world will weep
To see me lower it into the deep.
I'll carry the coffin.

Who'll sing a psalm?

Me, says the tractor, with my gear grinding glottle
I'll plough up the stubble and sing through my throttle.
I'll sing the psalm.

Who'll toll the bell?

Me, says the robin, my song in October
Will tell the still gardens the leaves are over.
I'll toll the bell.

Ted Hughes

Whistlestop!

> ### Word Game
> Proper names of places can be very strange. Look through an atlas or book of maps and collect names you like the sound of. Say them out loud and hear the rhythms. Group the words with the same rhythm together and create a train journey. Chant it out loud.

Diss, Marsh,
Sheepwash, Sheerness,
Norwich, Ipswich, Nantwich, Cambridge,
Poole,
Liverpool, Ullapool, Hartlepool, Pontypool,
Galloway, Londonderry, Templemartin,
Chester, Leicester, Gloucester, Cirencester,
Winchester, Manchester, Dorchester, Colchester, Chichester,
Wokingham, York,
Walsingham, Larne,
Leamington, Arne,
Gillingham, Fring,
Willingham, Tring,
Prestonpans,
Piddletrenthide,
Market Harborough,
Bedwellty,
Banff,
Eton, Oxford,
Invergarry, Invergowrie,
Inverary, Tipperary,
Canterbury, Netherbury, Bucklebury, Pontesbury,
Axminster, Sturminster, Yetminster, Upminster,
Slough, Limerick,
Ash,
Neath,
Meeth.

Night Mail

This is the Night Mail crossing the Border,
Bringing the cheque and the postal order,

Letters for the rich, letters for the poor
The shop at the corner, the girl next door.

Pulling up Beattock, a steady climb:
The gradient's against her, but she's on time.

Past cotton-grass and moorland boulder,
Shovelling white steam over her shoulder,

Snorting noisily, she passes
Silent miles of wind-bent grasses.

Birds turn their heads as she approaches,
Stare from bushes at her blank-faced coaches.

Sheep-dogs cannot turn her course;
They slumber on with paws across.

In the farm she passes no one wakes,
But a jug in a bedroom gently shakes.

Dawn freshens. Her climb is done.
Down towards Glasgow she descends,
Towards the steam tugs yelping down a glade of cranes,
Towards the fields of apparatus, the furnaces
Set on the dark plain like gigantic chessmen.
All Scotland waits for her:
In dark glens, beside pale-green lochs,
Men long for news.

Letters of thanks, letters from banks,
Letters of joy from girl and boy,
Receipted bills and invitations
To inspect new stock or to visit relations,
And applications for situations,
And timid lovers' declarations,
And gossip, gossip from all the nations,
News circumstantial, news financial,
Letters with holiday snaps to enlarge in,
Letters with faces scrawled in the margin,
Letters from uncles, cousins and aunts,
Letters to Scotland from the South of France,
Letters of condolence to Highlands and Lowlands,
Written on paper of every hue,
The pink, the violet, the white and the blue,
The chatty, the catty, the boring, the adoring,
The cold and official and the heart's outpouring,
Clever, stupid, short and long,
The typed and the printed and the spelt all wrong.

Thousands are still asleep,
Dreaming of terrifying monsters
Or a friendly tea beside the band in Cranston's or Crawford's:
Asleep in working Glasgow, asleep in well-set Edinburgh,
Asleep in granite Aberdeen,
They continue their dreams,
But shall wake soon and hope for letters,
And none will hear the postman's knock
Without a quickening of the heart.
For who can bear to feel himself forgotten?

W. H. Auden

Oranges and Lemons

Oranges and lemons,
Say the bells of St Clement's.
You owe me five farthings,
Say the bells of St Martin's.
When will you pay me?
Say the bells of Old Bailey.
When I grow rich,
Say the bells of Shoreditch.
Pray, when will that be?
Say the bells of Old Stepney.
I'm sure I don't know,
Says the big bell of Bow.
Here comes a candle to light you to bed,
Here comes a chopper to chop off your head.

One potato, two potato, three potato, four,
Five potato, six potato, seven potato, more.

Who put the cookie in the cooking pot?
Number 2 put the cookie in the cooking pot.
Who me?
Yes, you.
Couldn't be.
Yes, you.
Number 4 put the cookie in the cooking pot.

Word Game

How many chants and playground rhymes can you collect? Say them out loud. Do you notice the rhythm, or beat, of them? Collect as many as you can.

Word Game

Make a collection of words that have interesting rhythms when you say them out loud. Many words have really good sounds.

You could work as a group and put your words together. Chant them out loud and make a machine. You could even do actions and make a group machine where you all repeat your own words and movement at the same time.

Machines

There is rhythm all around you.
- Listen to your heart beat.
- Listen to a clock ticking.
- Listen to the rain falling.
- Listen to machines.

Grumble	grumble	grumble	grumble
Tappety	tappety	tappety	tappety
Wheel	wheel	wheel	wheel
Round and round and round and round and			
Shiver	shiver	shiver	shiver
Bottlewasher	bottlewasher	bottlewasher	bottlewasher
Plug	—	plug	—
Hammer	down	hammer	down
Over and	over and	over and	over and
Repeat	repeat	repeat	repeat
—	groan	—	groan
Pink	—	—	—
—	—	—	Snatch
Screech	high	screech	high
copper	kettle	copper	kettle

To Plough and Sow, to Reap and Mow

Way, haul away, we'll haul away together,
Way, haul away, we'll haul away, Joe.
Way, haul away, we'll haul for better weather,
Way, haul away, we'll haul away, Joe.

Early every morning at seven o'clock
There were twenty terriers drilling at the rock,
The boss comes around and he says keep still
And come down heavy on your cast-iron drill,
And drill, ye terriers, drill.
Drill, ye terriers, drill.
You work all day for the sugar in your tea,
Down behind the railway.
Drill, ye terriers, drill,
And blast,
And fire!

> **Did You Know?** People used to make up songs to help them do rhythmic but often monotonous, boring jobs. Sailors made up sea shanties like 'Haul Away, Joe' to sing while they were hauling on ropes. The songs helped them to keep in time with each other. Many work songs originated in factories and farms. A number of songs come from the American cotton plantations where the workers were mainly Africans who had been sold into slavery. The songs helped them to do the back-breaking jobs and to keep their spirits up.

I'm gonna jump down, turn around,
Pick a bale o' cotton,
Gonna jump down, turn around,
Pick a bale a day.
Oh, Lordy, pick a bale o' cotton,
Oh, Lordy, pick a bale a day.

Nailer's Song (nail-makers of the Midlands)

'Ommer, 'ommer, 'ommer, clink, clink, clink,
Work all day without any drink;
Pudding on a Sunday without any fat:
Poor old nailers can't buy that.

Work

Poverty Knock (Cotton Mill Song)

Poverty, poverty knock,
My loom is a-sayin all day.
Poverty, poverty knock,
Gaffer's too skinny to pay.
Poverty, poverty knock,
Keepin' one eye on the clock.
I know I can guttle when I hear my shuttle go
Poverty, poverty knock.

Word Game
Make up a work song which has a strong rhythm and would help you to do a particular job, like chopping down trees, sweeping the floor, digging, milking a cow, or working on an assembly line in a factory.

Verse of The Morn is Black (Cotton/Silk Mill Song)

Oh the whistle is a-blowing, sleep my bonny bairn;
Oh the whistle is a-blowing, it's time for me to go.
Oh the wheels they go a-turning and the noise it makes thee scream;
There's a racing and a going and the hissing of the steam.

> **Word Game**
> Many sports have definite repeated rhythms too. You could write a rhythmic poem to echo the sounds of a sport, like running, hurdling, riding a horse, playing tennis, or rowing.

Sewing Machine

I'm faster, I'm faster than fingers,
    much faster.
No mistress can match me, no mistress
    nor master.
My bobbin is racing to feed in the
    thread,
Pink, purple, grey, green, lemon-yellow,
    or red.
My needle, my needle, my slim, sharp
    steel needle,
Makes tiny, neat stitches in trousers
    and dresses
And firmly my silver foot presses,
    it presses.
I'm faster, I'm faster than fingers,
    much faster.

Gwen Dunn

From How They Brought The Good News from Ghent to Aix

I sprang to the stirrup, and Joris, and he;
I galloped, Dirck galloped, we galloped all three.
"God speed!" cried the watch, as the gatebolts undrew;
"Speed!" echoed the wall to us galloping through;
Behind shut the postern, the lights sank to rest
And into the midnight we galloped abreast.

Robert Browning

Orange, Silver, Sausage

Some words I've studied for a time
Like orange, silver, sausage;
But as for finding them a rhyme,
I'm at a total lossage!

Colin West

Word Game
Other words have many rhymes.
How many words can you find that rhyme with these?

tea	station	stall
sea	navigation	squall
me	operation	fall

Did You Know? There are some everyday words that do not have any other words that rhyme with them, like 'orange', 'silver', 'sausage' and 'secret'. Can you think of any more?

Dad and the Cat and the Tree

This morning a cat got
Stuck in our tree.
Dad said, 'Right, just
Leave it to me.'

The tree was wobbly,
The tree was tall.
Mum said, 'For goodness
Sake don't fall.'

'Fall?' scoffed Dad,
'A climber like me?
Child's play, this is!
You wait and see.'

He got out the ladder
From the garden shed.
It slipped. He landed
In the flower bed.

'Never mind,' said Dad,
Brushing the dirt
Off his hair and his face
And his trousers and his shirt,

'We'll try Plan B. Stand
Out of the way!'
Mum said, 'Don't fall
Again, O.K.?'

'Fall again?' said Dad.
'Funny joke!'
Then he swung himself up
On a branch. It broke.

Dad landed wallop
Back on the deck.
Mum said, 'Stop it,
You'll break your neck!'

'Rubbish!' said Dad.
'Now we'll try Plan C.
Easy as winking
To a climber like me!'

Then he climbed up high
On the garden wall.
Guess what?
He *didn't* fall!

He gave a great leap
And he landed flat
In the crook of the tree-trunk
Right on the cat!

The cat gave a yell
And sprang to the ground,
Pleased as Punch to be
Safe and sound.

So it's smiling and smirking,
Smug as can be,
But poor old Dad's
Still stuck up the tree!

Kit Wright

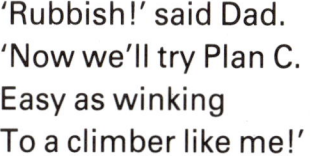

Rhyme

Did You Know? Poems do NOT have to rhyme! If you want to use rhyme in your poems you must make sure the rhyming words are suitable for what you want to say. Don't just choose any old rhyme! Otherwise you get something like this:

> One evening in the month of June
> I sat beneath the silvery moon
> And hummed a favourite little tune
> And tried to eat a stewed prune.

This does not tell us very much of great interest. The rhymes (June, moon, tune and prune) have taken over the poem.

Word Game

With a partner play RHYME TENNIS.
You serve a word to your partner who must return a rhyming word. *You* rhyme back and you keep the rally going until one of you cannot think of a rhyme. Score as in tennis. You must not use the same word twice.

		Umpire	
Service	chance		
			dance
	France		
			lance
	advance		
			prance
	glance		
			? Eee!
		15–LOVE	
Service	stepped		
			crept
	leapt		
			kept
	? Oh, No!		
		15–ALL	
Service	field		
			shield
	yield		
			peeled
	? Ugh!		
		15–30	

Service	music		
		?	Aah!
	30–ALL		
Service	laughter		
			rafter
	after		
			dafter
	? Ooh!		
	30–40		
Service	term		
			worm
	squirm		
			perm
	germ		
		?	Oh!
	DEUCE		
Service	voice		
			choice
	rejoice		
		?	Help!
	ADVANTAGE SERVER		
Service	language		
		?!!	(Language!)
	GAME		

51

Mime the Rhyme

Word Game – MIME THE RHYME
You need two teams for this game. One team secretly decides on *one* word. Make sure it is a word which has plenty of rhymes, like 'bed'. Tell the other team a word which rhymes with your word. If it were 'bed', you might say, "Our word rhymes with 'bread'." The members of the other team must try to guess your word. They do this by thinking of other words that rhyme with 'bread' and miming these words. The first team must identify the word being mimed and say it. If 'dead' is being mimed, they must say "No, it is not 'dead'." If they cannot guess the mime they lose a point. Each team starts with 10 points and loses one every time it guesses wrongly. The game continues until one team loses all its points, or the mimed word is correct.

From Mrs Worthington

Don't put your daughter on the stage,
  Mrs Worthington,
Don't put your daughter on the stage,
The profession is overcrowded
And the struggle's pretty tough,
And admitting the fact
She's burning to act,
That isn't quite enough.
She has nice hands, to give the wretched
  girl her due,
But don't you think her bust is too
Developed for her age,
I repeat
Mrs Worthington,
Sweet
Mrs Worthington,
Don't put your daughter on the stage.

Noel Coward

King Foo Foo

King Foo Foo sat upon his throne
Dressed in his royal closes,
While all around his courtiers stood
With clothes-pegs on their noses.

'This action strange,' King Foo Foo said,
'My mind quite discomposes,
Though vulgar curiosity
A good king never shoses.'

But to the court it was as clear
As poetry or prose is:
King Foo Foo had not had a bath
Since goodness only knowses.

But one fine day the Fire Brigade
Rehearsing with their hoses
(To Handel's Water Music played
With many puffs and bloses)

Quite failed the water to control
In all its ebbs and floses
And simply drenched the King with sev-
Eral thousand gallon doses.

'A debt to keep his courtiers gay
A monarch surely owses,
And deep within my royal breast
A sporting heart reposes.'

So now each night it's water bright
The Fire Brigade disposes
Over a King who smells as sweet
As all the royal roses.

Charles Causley

Half-time

Did You Know? There is another kind of rhyming called HALF-RHYME.
Full rhymes are like 'dine' and fine'.
HALF-RHYMES are like 'dine' and 'done'
or 'dine' and 'lime'.
'dine' and 'done' share the same sounds 'd' and 'n'.
'dine' and 'lime' share the same sound 'i'.
This is very useful when you write a poem.
It means you have more words to choose from if you want to rhyme.

Robin

With a bonfire throat,
Legs of twig,
A dark brown coat,
The inspector robin
Comes where I dig.

Military man
With a bright eye
And a wooden leg,
He must scrounge and beg
Now the summer's by:

Beg at the doors,
Scrounge in the gardens,
While daylight *lessens*
And the grass *glistens*
And the ground hardens.

The toads have their vaults,
The squirrels their *money*,
The swifts their *journey*;
For him the earth's *anger*,
The taste of *hunger*.

And his unfrightened song
For the impending snows
Is also for the rose
And for the great Armada
And the Phoenician trader
And the last missile raider –
It's the only one he knows.

Hal Summers

Rhyme-time

Word Game Play RHYME TENNIS using HALF-RHYMES (see page 50). You can also make a word chain with a group of people or on your own using HALF-RHYMES.

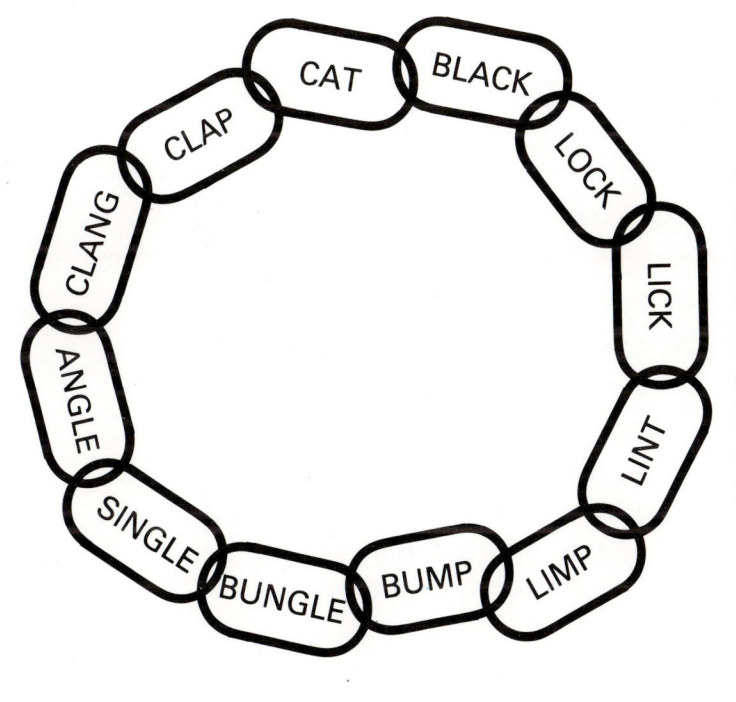

Did You Know? Rhymes do *not* have to go at the ends of lines. A rhyme is a word that chimes the same sound. You can put them in the middle of lines if you like. This poem uses HALF-RHYMES and INTERNAL RHYME (rhymes in the middle of lines).

To Be Sold

Metal meets metal, the last noise.
Not seeing, only hearing the *rain*
Drill down on the corrugated *tin*,
The calf inhales the *smell* of his ancestors
Who know the place *well*
Like a criminal knowing his *cell*.
Winds play tunes through holes in the
                                     walls,
The orphan baby whose mother is gone
And she *calls*.

Zak Hall

Rhyme-time

I know that poems do not have to rhyme,
And yet I've always liked to hear words chime.
I've noticed, too, that in the world's design
Rhymes play their part, occurring all the time,
Not just in sounds but in the way the fine
Gestures of a tiny plant will mime
In miniature the flourish of a pine,
Proud and lonely on the hill's skyline;
Or how the bright refulgence of moonshine
Is almost echoed in the sheen of lime;
The way the hawthorn foams, a paradigm
For spindrift blossom on the dancing brine.

Oh yes, it's true, all poems do not rhyme
But of the things that I will treasure, nine
Times out of ten, the sounds and objects sign
Themselves on memory and warmly twine
Around the heart and rhythms of the spine
Through using chime and echo.
                            It's no crime –
As verbal savages in grime and slime
Of their poetic darkness whine – to climb
To transcendental heights or try to mine
Deep in mysteries equally sublime
By rungs or shafts of rhyme. I know that I'm
Old fashioned but I'd never care to sign
A contract that debars the chiming line.
Finally, I ask, what sweeter rhyme
Than your close heartbeat keeping time with mine?

Vernon Scannell

Mutton Pies

> **Did You Know?** The London Cockneys invented a form of rhyming language so that other people couldn't understand what they were saying. It is called Rhyming Slang and uses expressions that rhyme with the word, instead of the word itself. Instead of saying 'eyes', they would say 'mutton pies'. Often they even shortened the rhyming slang and would only say the first word. So, 'going up the apples' means 'going up the apples and pears' (stairs).

Rabbit and Pork, Rhyming Talk

All afloat	coat
Barnet Fair	hair
Bread and cheese	knees
Cain and Abel	table
Cribbage pegs	legs
North and south	mouth
East and west	breast
Frog and toad	main road
German flutes	pair of boots
Ginger pop	cop
Henry Meville	Devil
Hampstead Heath	teeth
I suppose	nose
Jenny Lee	flea
Jonah's whale	tail
Jumbo's trunk	drunk
Lump of lead	head
Mutton pies	eyes
Noah's Ark	lark
Plates of meat	feet
Rank and riches	breeches
Round the houses	trousers
Storm and strife	wife
Sugar and honey	money
Sunny south	mouth
Take a fright	night
Turtle doves	pair of gloves
Two-foot rule	fool
Walter Joyce	voice

Traditional English

Tottie

As she walked along the street
With her little plates of meat
And the summer sunshine falling on her golden Barnet Fair,
Bright as angels from the skies
Were her dark blue Mutton Pies;
In my East and West Dan Cupid shot a shaft and left it there.

She'd a Grecian I suppose
And of Hampstead Heath two rows,
In her Sunny South they glistened like two pretty strings of pearls,
Down upon my bread and cheese
Did I drop and murmur, 'Please
Be my storm and strife, dear Tottie, O, you darlingest of girls.'

Then a bow wow by her side
Who 'til then had stood and tried
A Jenny Lee to banish, which was on his Jonah's Whale,
Gave a hydrophobia bark,
She cried, 'What a Noah's Ark,'
And right through my rank and riches did my cribbage pegs assail.

Ere her bull dog I could stop
She had called a ginger pop
Who said, 'What the Henry Meville do you think you're doing there?'
And I heard as off I slunk,
'Why the fellow's Jumbo's trunk.'
And the Walter Joyce was Tottie's with the golden Barnet Fair. . . .

Traditional English

Word Game
Write a story using Rhyming Slang. Make up your own new rhyming phrases.

Glossary of Terms

Alliteration	a group of words that begin with the same sound coming together, *e.g.* **F**ull **f**athom **f**ive thy **f**ather lies.
Similes	saying something *is like* something else, *e.g.* as light as a feather, a voice like thunder.
Metaphor	comparing two things by saying one *is* the other, *e.g.* The moon is a round of cheese.
Half-rhyme	words that sound similar but do not rhyme exactly, *e.g.* lake and leak, time and tide.
Full Rhyme	words that chime together, rhyming exactly, *e.g.* cat and mat, mouse and house.

Index of Poems (Titles and First Lines)

A Famous Fish Factor Found himself, 8
All of my attics used to sing, 34
As she walked along the street, 58
Barbra looks longingly at the lamp shade, 31
Beach, The, 18
Belly stuffed with dust and fluff, 18
Class, The, 30
Cleaning Ladies, 18
Dad and the Cat and the Tree, 48
Don't put your daughter on the stage, 52
Early every morning at seven o'clock, 44
Far Famed Fairy Tale of Fenella, The, 8
Fly, The, 14
Frogs, 15
Frogs sit more solid, 15
Funeral, 31
He needs / A coat like thick brown moss, 13
He needs / A head like a snake, a neck like a drake, 13
How a Good Greyhound is Shaped, 13
How large unto the tiny fly, 14
How They Brought The Good News from Ghent to Aix, 46
How to Make a Bear, 13
I know that poems do not have to rhyme, 56
I often wonder why, oh why, 22
I sprang to the stirrup, and Joris, and he, 46
I want to be a wallaby, 7
I was round and small like a pearl, 26
I Will Give my Love an Apple, 27
I will give my love an apple, without e'er a core, 27
If I look within the mirror, 24
I'm faster, I'm faster than fingers, 46

I'm gonna jump down, turn around, 44
Imagine, 14
Imagine a snail, 14
In marble walls as white as milk, 26
In the pond in the park, 20
In This City . . . , 32
In this city, perhaps a street, 32
Inquisitiveness, 22
Intelligence Test, 23
It is in the rock but not in the stone, 25
It's Winter, it's Winter, 33
It's winter, it's winter, it's wonderful winter, 33
King Foo Foo, 53
King Foo Foo sat upon his throne, 53
Leaves, 38
London Bus Conductor's Prayer, The, 37
Metal meets metal, the last noise, 55
Mirror Poem, 24
Monday's child is fair of face, 28
Morn is Black, The, 45
Mrs Worthington, 52
My breast is puffed up and my neck is swollen, 27
My first is in book but not in cover, 26
My girl's a corker, 12
Neddie Noodle nipped his Neighbour's Nutmegs, 7
Night Mail, 40
Nutter, 18
Oh dear, what can the matter be?, 36
Oh the whistle is a-blowing, 45
'Ommer, 'ommer, 'ommer, clink, clink, clink, 44
One for sorrow, two for joy, 28

One potato, two potato, 42
One waggly walrus won a wet wager, 10
Oranges and lemons, 42
Orange, Silver, Sausage, 47
Our Father who art in Hendon, 37
Please, how does one spell definite?, 22
Poverty Knock, 45
Poverty, poverty knock, 45
Questions, 22
Rhyme-time, 56
Riddle of the Sphinx, The, 25
Robin, 54
Sea, The, 19
Sewing Machine, 46
Solomon Grundy, born on Monday, 28
Some words I've studied for a time, 47
Song of a House, The, 34
Summer, 19
Summer is a cigarette, 19
Swan swam over the sea, 7
Ten-ton Tina's staring, 30
The beach is a quarter of golden fruit, 18
The moon's a big white football, 18
The sea is a hungry dog, 19
There once was a very small window, 35
This is the house that Jack built, 29
This is the key of the kingdom, 33
This is the night mail crossing the border, 40
This morning a cat got, 48
To Be Sold, 55
Tottie, 58

Twinkle, twinkle, little bat, 36
Water Picture, 20
Way, haul away, we'll haul away together, 44
'What do you use your eyes for?', 23
What has one voice, 25
Who put the cookie in the cooking pot?, 42
Who's killed the leaves?, 38
Window, 35
With a bonfire throat, 54
You're the Top!, 16
You're the top!, 16

Index of Poets

Auden, W. H., 40
Beswick, Kefi, 31
Browning, Robert, 46
Brownjohn, Alan, 32
Carroll, Lewis, 36
Causley, Charles, 53
Coward, Noel, 52
de la Mare, Walter, 14
Dunn, Gwen, 46
Egan, Roland, 14
Hall, Zak, 55
Hart-Smith, W., 18
Hughes, Ted, 38
MacCaig, Norman, 15
Meyers, Rachel, 30
Nathan, Mark, 19
Porter, Cole, 16
Reeves, James, 19
Scannell, Vernon, 23, 56
Summers, Hal, 54
Swenson, May, 20
Webber, Steve, 35
West, Colin, 7, 22, 47
Wilson, Raymond, 22
Wright, Kit, 18, 24, 33, 48